There's a wonderful walk along the canal that takes you from Castlefield to Piccadilly Village, with points along the way where you can stop for food or toilets. You could jog the whole length in a handful of minutes or walk it there and back comfortably in just over an hour. The walk follows the towpath almost all of the way, and consequently you are away from the noise and the hustle of the city streets - and it's surprising how being a few yards away from the roar can give you a new dimension to the city. It's quiet and still along the towpath in complete contrast to the mad rush above you, and whether you walk the whole way or just ramble along a bit of it in your lunch hour, it's a welcome break from the rat-race, for a while at least.

Because it's almost all on the level it's easy walking, though stiletto heels and pencil skirts are not recommended - even for women. It's great for families with kids and for those whose hill-climbing days, though not over are perhaps not as frequent, and there are some facilities (though not nearly enough) for the disabled.

There is one reservation that I must make. We don't live in particularly good times and I wouldn't recommend that women or children walk the more secluded lengths of the walk alone. The undercroft at London Road is a good example of what I mean: there is lighting and it's perfectly safe underfoot, and in fact it's quite exciting to walk the canal bank under the roads and buildings, but it is a little dark and the ideal place for the lurker and the city shark - I need say no more.

The Development Corporation is employing Urban Rangers to patrol Castlefield and the canals. They are most welcome.

The walk can be done as a linear trek - it's about three miles from Castlefield to Piccadilly Village and back. On the other hand you can walk the towpath as far as Canal Street, leave the city centre for something to eat, then take the new Metrolink service back to Deansgate and Castlefield. The variations are many, and whichever way you choose there's so much to see and do, It's a walk I've done over and over again.

This little guide is intended to give you a taste of some of the interesting sights around Castlefield and along the Rochdale Canal. There are some things we've had to leave out because of space, and no doubt there are others you'll find that I've missed - well that's the whole point of it all really, isn't it?

Old Roman Manchester

Roman Castlefield

Castlefield itself is the core of old Roman Manchester. Some of the remains of the Roman fort and a reconstructed portion of the wall can be seen just off Liverpool Street and are well worth a wander round. I particularly like the garden with plants that are said to have been brought here by the Romans, box, fig tree and ivy. The old Roman name for the city is *Mamucium,* which like Mam Tor in Derbyshire could mean either a 'breast shaped hill' or a place special to the mother goddess of the Brigantes, the local Celtic tribe the Romans were so keen to subdue. They never really did subdue them (I like to think that this reflects our northern cussedness) and were forced to treat with them instead. At one time there were eight hundred foot soldiers and cavalry within the fort; and you can imagine how many people, farmers, butchers, tavern-keepers, pedlars and others, would have to come in from the surrounding countryside to look after the army's needs. It is reckoned that the *vicus*, the surrounding civilian village, would have held more than two thousand people, so this little spot over the Irwell must have been a noisy and bustling place at its height in around 250AD.

The fort was manned by soldiers from several parts of the Roman Empire, amongst them a cohort of Frisians (people not cows). It commanded the river crossing over the Irwell on the Roman road from Chester to York and it also connected with forts at Glossop, and Castleshaw near Oldham. I always try and imagine what life was like then: there would have been nothing much here of course, just the fort on its mound above the river crossing, and the tents and shelters of travellers and camp followers huddled close by. But unless the weather was much different or they were made of hardier stuff those Roman soldiers must have almost froze to death, dressed in their short leather skirts and sandals, standing on guard-duty staring out towards the river, with the cold mist of January sticking its icy fingers up their togas.

Castlefield has a number of good pubs such as the White Lion, the Commercial and the Oxnoble, and the Old Pack Horse across at Knott Mill. There is Dimitri's Deli in the arcade of the old City Hall, while the Castlefield Hotel has an excellent bar, restaurant and a snack bar in its sports area; so there are plenty of places you can fuel up before the off, or warm up on your return. The Castlefield Hotel, by the way, also has excellent facilities for the disabled and offers a good way down to the basin for wheelchairs.

• For further information on disabled facilities see page 26

Castlefield Today

The museum at Castlefield is just magic. I can spend hours there, particularly in the Power section looking at the massive mill engines and the Beyer and Peacock loco made in Gorton, Manchester, that used to drag iron ore across the Drakensberg Mountains of South Africa. It took two days to steam it up and its fire grate was so big and hungry that a separate steam engine had to be fired first to work the machinery that fed coal into the firebox. The aerospace section has a brilliant collection of flying machines from the massive Shackleton early warning aircraft to a tiny micro-lite. Back in the main building again there is a gas gallery, electricity gallery, an underground sewer and 'The Making of Manchester' Exhibition, and on Sundays and bank holidays you can ride on a steam train up and down the maze of railway lines in the museum grounds. There are two excellent cafes and a wonderful 'hands on' section for kids and non-kids. The museum buildings are magical caves of brass and steam, aluminium and glass, and I just wish there had been something as good as this around when I was a nipper.

Round the corner from the museum is Granada Studios Tour, where there's a huge amount to see from the original Coronation Street complete with the Rover's Return where the ghosts of Ena Sharples and Albert Tatlock walk twice nightly, to the scale model of the Houses of Parliament used in *First Among Equals* and the sets for the Sherlock Holmes series. A river bus goes from Granadaland up the Irwell as far as Salford Quays and a new themed hotel will be opening in October 1992 as part of the complex. In this 'Hollywood by the Irwell' the Motion Master Cinema pays tribute to film-making of the 21st Century: it is one of the most advanced cinemas in the world, with computer-controlled seats that move with the action at speeds of more than 5ft per second. There are plans for a new pedestrian bridge across the river together with walkways and landscaped gardens, and there are also plans to include some of the underground canals that thread beneath the studios in future developments.

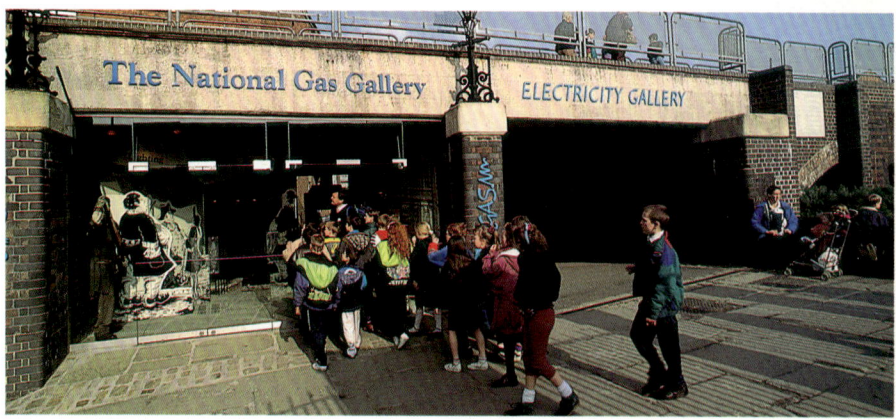

4

The Canal Basin

The walk begins at the Staffordshire steps by the Castlefield Hotel. Once down at canal level you can see to your left the open space earmarked for an outdoor events area where concerts and light shows will be held, while to the right is the old Potato Wharf where new canal arms are being dug out and safe moorings provided to turn the area into a lively marina. A youth hostel is also planned.

Follow the towpath along the canal arm, cross one of the new cast-iron bridges and go under the arches of the Castlefield viaducts, which carry the new Metrolink from Altrincham as well as serving the usual traffic of goods trains, inter-city and local services. The massive iron piers support the last of the four viaducts to be built at Castlefield, an amazing symbol of Victorian engineering confidence. The building of this viaduct and the Great Northern Railway warehouse on Deansgate cost more than a million pounds in the 1890s and meant the clearance of a whole area of housing in Alport Town. Hundreds of working class families were evicted without compensation, although the developers saw it as an 'enlightened form of slum clearance.'

It is in the basin beyond the piers of the viaduct that the Rochdale and Bridgewater Canals meet. Completed in 1764, the Bridgewater was the first 'cut' navigation in the country: previous to that rivers had been used for navigation but the new industrial age wanted faster, more reliable forms of water transport and the Canal Duke gave it to them, driving canals into the heart of his mines at Worsley, right up to the coal face.

When the Rochdale Canal Company opened their canal in 1805 it completed the waterways link between the North Sea and the Irish Sea. It was a massive project, akin to the building of the M62 in

our own times. Hollingworth Lake near Rochdale was created to feed the canal, and on the moors near Blackstone Edge the great reservoirs of Light Hazles and Warland, where the Pennine Way skirts the valley edge, were built for the same purpose. At first the Duke of Bridgewater refused to allow the Rochdale to link with his canal because he was afraid that he might lose trade, but then, realising that other companies might drive canals through to the Rochdale anyway, he changed his mind - though he still drove a hard bargain. Every boat entering the Bridgewater from the Rochdale had to pay a toll and all water flowing out of the Rochdale into the Bridgewater was his for free. Since seven million gallons a day flowed down the Rochdale because of its ninety two locks the Duke came off pretty well in the deal.

During the summer the *Worsley Packet* makes short pleasure cruises up the Bridgewater to the Ship Canal from the basin and it's well worth a trip.

Castlefield

The Canal Basin

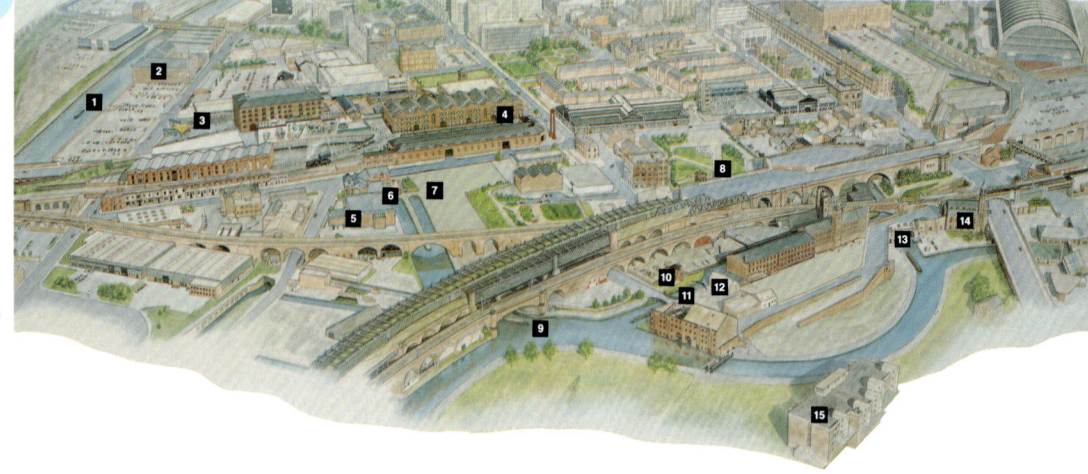

KEY
1. River Irwell
2. Victoria and Albert Hotel
3. Granada Studios Tour
4. Museum of Science and Industry
5. Castlefield Hotel
6. Staffordshire Steps
7. Site for Castlefield Events Area
8. Reconstructed Roman Fort
9. Bridgewater Canal
10. Lock-Keeper's Cottage
11. Rochdale Canal
12. Dukes 92
13. Grocers' Warehouse
14. Congregational Chapel
15. Castle Quay

Beyond the massive piers of the viaduct stand the old stone bridge and Dukes 92, a new pub developed from the stables of the old Merchants warehouse of 1827, which is across the road. This is the oldest surviving example of the great canal warehouses of the last century, and although it's in a pretty poor state there are plans to turn it into a hotel. Dukes 92 itself serves real ale and excellent cheese and pâte lunches, and is named after the Canal Duke and the nearby lock, the 92nd on the Rochdale Canal from Yorkshire.

If you stand on the stone bridge and look down you will notice that the lock has short arms and is opened by a system of chains and wheels. That is because the lock is so close to the bridge that there isn't enough room to open a full set of arms. If you look closely at some of the mushroom-shaped mooring bollards on the towpath you'll notice that one of them in particular has a deeply grooved stem: the grooves were worn in it by the rubbing of countless ropes as the horse-drawn barges were moored up waiting to go through the lock.

When I was a boy I was told the story of a man walking along the canal who comes upon a bargee carefully and slowly chiselling two grooves in the underside of a bridge over the canal.

'What're you doing that for pal?' he asks in his best Manchester accent

'It's the horse,' says the bargee, 'His ears touch the underneath of the bridge and he doesn't like it so he won't go through. I'm making two troughs for 'em.'

'Why don't you get a shovel and dig a trench in the towpath, it'd be a lot quicker?' the man asks.

The bargee gives him a withering look. 'You great cloth-head, it's not his legs that are too long it's his ears!'

The Canal Basin

The lock-keeper's house facing Dukes 92 is built on a skew so that the lock-keeper could keep an eye on his whole 'pound', the basin and both of its feeder canals, from one point. It was his job to collect tolls for the Duke and he must have been kept fairly busy running up and down making sure that nobody 'did a runner'. It's worth walking on past the pub, keeping it on your left and rounding the corner along Castle Street. All this area is being well developed and though some of the wildlife moved out when the work started we're hoping that the kingfisher and heron that were seen in the silted-up reed beds and choked arms will return one day to keep the swans and ducks company. The huge building ahead of you is the old Middle Warehouse of around 1830, now called Castle Quay by the Manchester Ship Canal Company, who have turned it into flats and offices and reopened the old canal arm. They've made a splendid feature of the shipping holes where the barges used to sail right in to load and unload. You'll also see the 'Van Gogh Bridge' (no, Van Gogh didn't design it when he worked for Manchester Council - it just looks like the one he painted at Arles). Along Castle Street is the old Bass Warehouse, and next door Gail House is now called Eastgate, because that's where the east gate of the old Roman fort used to be. At the end is Grocers' Wharf and the tunnels where the barges

took the coal to be hauled up to the level of the road above.

Many of these buildings are being refurbished, and in fact that is one of the most exciting aspects of this whole walk, the feeling that what was once nothing more than industrial dereliction, even though it has lost its original purpose, is being brought back to new life without being gentrified or turned into a theme park. The whole area will eventually be a mix of offices, homes, retail and leisure that should have something of the air of an urban village, and most excitingly people will once again be living in the heart of the city.

The Congregational Chapel above the canal was built in the 1850s (it was designed by Edward Walter, architect of the Free Trade Hall) and, like a number of Manchester buildings, it reflects the influence of Italy on the architectural styles of the day. It is built of 'Italianate red brick' and wouldn't look out of place in Siena. Now Pete Waterman has turned it into a recording studio.

Returning to Dukes 92 we now follow the Rochdale Canal towpath towards Deansgate and Oxford Road.

Canal Street to Albion Street

As you travel eastward you'll pass some grotty looking buildings on the opposite bank, soon to be redeveloped; and to the right the back of the warehouses that are already being refurbished. Ahead of you are the great, bowed, cast-iron arches of the railway bridge, supported on the red sandstone bedrock.

The canal was cut into this bedrock by teams of navvies using 'hand-draulics', i.e. gunpowder, pick, shovel and barrow. They were hard men and their name 'navvies' comes from 'navigations', the old name for the canals. They were migrant workers, many of them Irish and Scots, and they went wherever canal work was being done, living in shanty towns that sprang up around the diggings, working hard and living hard. Like any other army they had their followers, pedlars and victuallers, ballad sellers and quack medicine men. The navvies had no names other than the nicknames they travelled by, like Banjo Jack, Roaring Tommy and Scots Mick, and when they died they were often buried there and then in the ground at the side of the cut. When they married there was no church or parson, so they joined hands and jumped over a broomstick - the old Northern expression 'living over the brush', used of a couple living together who aren't married, dates from this time.

The bridge in front of you was built by the second wave of navvies, the railway navvies, many of them the same men who had worked on the cut. They were part of that second great industrial revolution, the Victorian Railway Age, that itself was to bring about the end of the canals as trade routes. There was angry and voluble opposition when the railway bridge was built because it meant the destruction of the last remains of the Roman fort, and it is said that the castellated towers at either end of the bridge were built as a sop to the protesters.

On the opposite bank you can see the narrow wooden jetties and moorings of what was once an old coal wharf but is now a landscaped area, one of the wildlife refuges along the route. In the summer you can see reed-mace and bur-reed growing here and ivy clings to the massive stones. Interestingly some of the plants here may have been brought in as seeds in Roman times. Notice an arm of the canal vanishing in a tunnel cut into the solid bedrock.

Just beyond Deansgate Tunnel above the canal is another lock-keeper's house, once derelict but now happily rescued by a group of architects to use as their own offices.

Central Station was a haunt of mine in childhood. That and Victoria-Exchange and London Road (Piccadilly as it is now called) were my stamping grounds as a train spotter when the greatest pleasure you got was to buy a penny platform ticket and run along the platform with all the other boys shouting 'It's a namer !!!' as some beast of steam, its great lungs booming, would come hissing and roaring into the station in a cloud of black smoke and white steam. Entirely against the law the drivers would let handfuls of kids on to the footplate and even give them a run up and down the platform if they were shunting on to a line of carriages. Now Central Station is the G-Mex Centre, its single-span roof one of the great engineering achievements of the Railway Age, while underneath it is an underground city of cobbled ways and brick-arched caverns. You could leave the canal here for a look at the station and the wonderful Midland hotel opposite, built by the Midland Railway Company in 1903 to serve the station when Manchester was at the height of its powers as the world's premier cloth city 'Cottonopolis'. The hotel, which was restored to much of its Cotton Town glory by the Holiday Inn group, does excellent afternoon teas.

One of the fascinating things about this walk is that for almost all its length you travel through the heart of the cotton warehousing and business areas of the world's first industrial city. Not far from the Midland Hotel is the Cotton Exchange - 'the biggest room in the world' - where the trading prices are still there to be seen high on the wall exactly as they were when trading ceased on the very last day of 1968. Today it houses the Royal Exchange Theatre.

12

A Birds Eye View of the Walk

- **A.** The Staffordshire Steps
- **B.** Museum of Science and Industry
- **C.** G-Mex
- **D.** Castlefield Hotel
- **E.** Castlefield Viaducts
- **F.** Dukes 92
- **G.** The Congregational Chapel
- **H.** Midland Hotel
- **I.** Hacienda
- **J.** The Peveril of the Peak
- **K.** The Cornerhouse
- **L.** The Palace Theatre
- **M.** Manchester City Art Gallery
- **N.** Manto Bar
- **O.** Chinatown
- **P.** Lock-Keepers Cottage
- **Q.** Magistrates Court
- **R.** Ducie Street Warehouse
- **S.** La Peniche
- **T.** Piccadilly Village

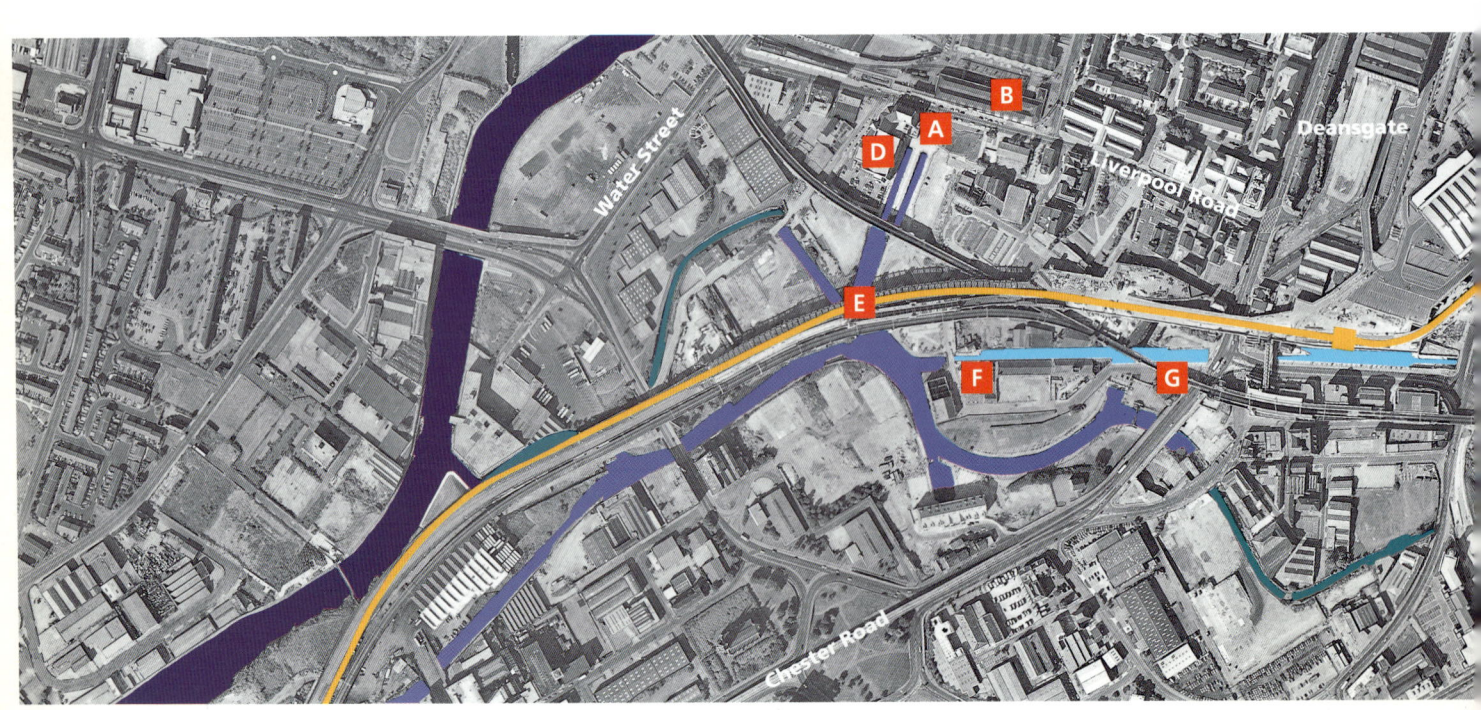

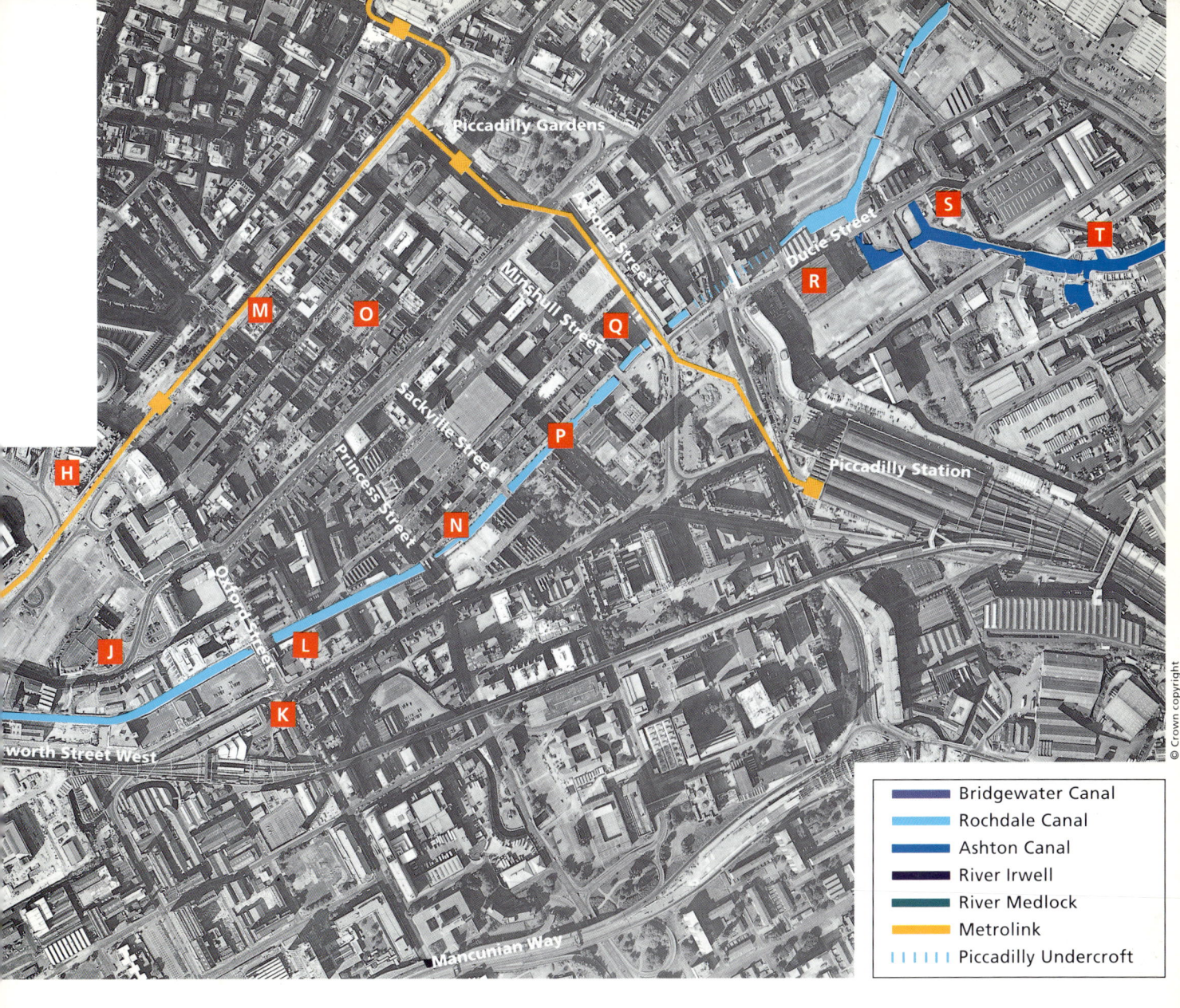

Albion Street to Oxford Street

Beyond Albion Street to your left as you emerge again into the light is Albion Wharf with four mock Graeco-Victorian pillars which are 'symbolic of the fragmentation of Post-Modernist architecture' (so now you know). In front of them is the Briton's Protection, which was given its unusual name at least 150 years ago, although its listed interior is more turn-of-the-century. To your right is the wall of the Hacienda Night Club, where the 'Manchester Sound' (as journalists call it) was born. It is probably as well known worldwide as Liverpool's Cavern was in the 'sixties. A little further on you can see, to the left, Chepstow House and the site of Manchester's new international concert hall. An arm of the canal used to run from here under a bridge to the rear of Chepstow House and then on to the Irwell, to bring coal up from the river, and though the building of Central Station filled in much of it, this arm and the lower end, under Granada Studios, are still salvageable. The Bridgewater arm is going to be re-opened to take barges right into the heart of the concert hall centre itself. There will be a 2,400 seater concert hall that will become the new home for Manchester's world renowned Hallé Orchestra, a restaurant, a canal basin and a piazza, all situated just across from the G-Mex Centre and an easy walk from both Castlefield and Piccadilly as well as being served by Metrolink.

The Peveril of the Peak, a fine Edwardian pub with wonderful tiling, stands close by Chepstow House. The story is told that one evening, having drunk deeply if not wisely, a customer staggered out of the pub, crossed the road and fell headlong into the canal. Luckily it was in the days when policemen still walked the streets and a passing Bootle Street bobby dived in and hauled the drowning man to the side. Pulling him half out of the water he began giving him artificial respiration. Gallons of water poured out of the poor man together with a couple of perch, a gudgeon and two confused newts. Several people had witnessed the accident and one man, a nervous-looking type wearing a brown gaberdine and a trilby, approached the bobby.

'Excuse me,' he ventured, *'but could I just point out that you're doing it wrong?'*

The policeman understandably was not impressed. Still pumping pondweed and soggy chip-papers out of the poor wretch he shouted, *'D'you know anything about first aid?'*

'No,' the man answered truthfully.

'Well shut your cake-hole then... - sir, ' said the constable as he carried on pumping. Three small roach and half an old boot emerged next, followed by several more gallons of water, a porcupine quill float and the nameplate off a barge that had sunk in the previous winter storms. And still he pumped and still the muddy water came.

'Excuse me,' ventured the man again, ' you are doing it wrong you know.'

'Look, you just told me you know nothing about first aid!' snarled the irate, sweating and un-laughing policeman.

'I may not know anything about first-aid but I am a hydraulics engineer, and I know that if you don't get his bum out of the water you're going to pump the canal dry.'

Ahead of you as you walk you can see the tower of the Refuge Building, one of Manchester's great architectural triumphs - you may have seen it in the Valette painting of Oxford Street when Manchester seemed to have pea-soupers second only to London's. The steam pipe that follows the canal to your right used to carry heat to many of the buildings in the city and was part of a clever steam-heating scheme devised by the owners of Bloom Street Power Station. Barges could pull right up under the loading bay and off-load coal directly into the power station. On the other bank of the canal you can see the expansion bend of the pipe.

There is still a fair amount of dereliction here but nearly all of the sites are scheduled for redevelopment.

You'll find good food at The Cornerhouse, Coco's new Italian restaurant in a railway arch, at the Green Room and in the new Charterhouse Hotel in the Refuge Building. Unfortunately, as yet there is no access to Oxford Street so your way off the canal here is via Whitworth Street car park.

16

A village in the city

Oxford Street to Canal Street

Filled up again you go back the way you came to the towpath, which then follows the back wall of Manchester's Palace Theatre. Built as a music hall in the nineteenth century, it was in danger of closing not so long ago but now it is an important part of the city's artistic life. This part of the canal works its way by Bridgewater House, just across the road from one of the greatest warehouses in the city, India House, which as its name implies owed a lot to Empire trade and cotton. As a lad I often went there picking up rolls of cloth for an employer I worked for. Today it's one of several residential schemes using old textile warehouses that have turned the Whitworth Street area almost into a 'village in the city'.

If you are interested in Pre-Raphaelite art then one of the country's best collections is housed just a stride away in the Manchester City Art Gallery, where there's a tremendous amount to see and also excellent food in the gallery cafe.

Dominion House, another old cotton warehouse, is now a hotel and serves first class food just in case you didn't stop at Oxford Road. The New Union Pub was one of my haunts as a callow youth and then as now was an important part of Manchester's gay community life. It has some interesting stained glass windows commemorating the Union (as in the British Flag and Empire) and is a lively place, serving good hot food during the day and with music and a rave-up most nights of the week. The old Mechanic's Arms where I used to play the banjo is now the Churchill, and the Rembrandt, like some of its clients, has had several facelifts, but otherwise the old pubs of this area aren't much changed.

If you wanted to end the walk here you could travel a few hundred yards to Piccadilly and take the Metrolink back to Deansgate and Castlefield; or if you've got the time it's well worth leaving the canal for an excursion into Manchester's Chinatown, where you can see the Chinese Arch and gardens and where you can get some of the best Chinese food in Britain. At Chinese New Year this whole area is locked solid with people who have come to see the famous dancing dragon. But back to the canal.

The lock-keeper's house still used by the canals 'Lengthsman', is built across the canal itself here and shows how tight they were for space in those days - so tight that the towpath disappears and becomes part of the road at Canal Street, where our next section begins.

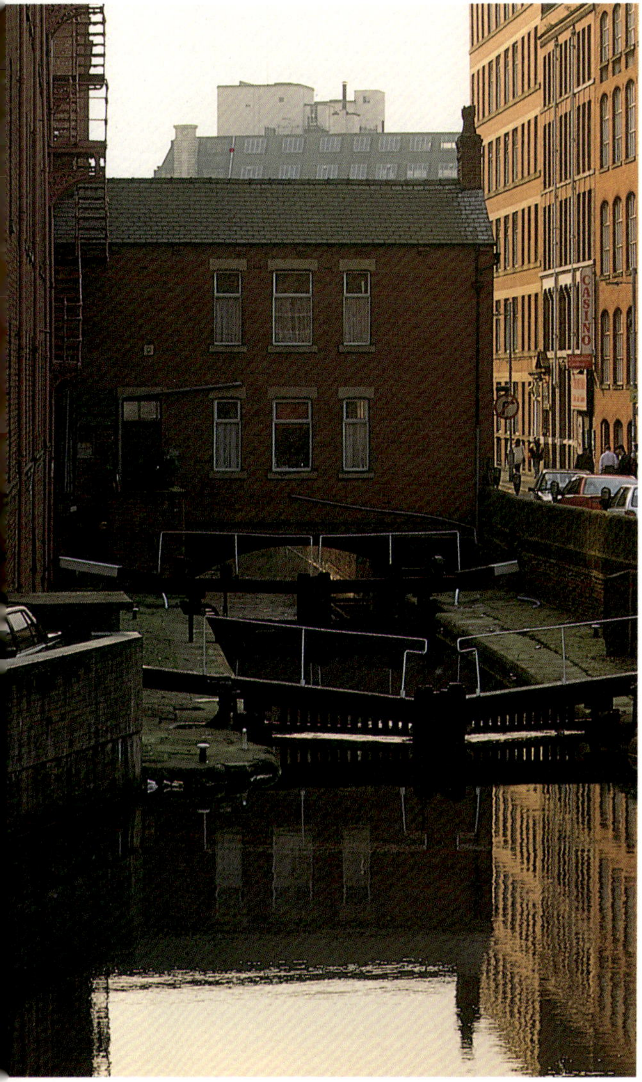
CASINO

曼徹斯特中國城
CHINA TOWN MANCHESTER

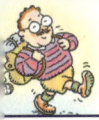

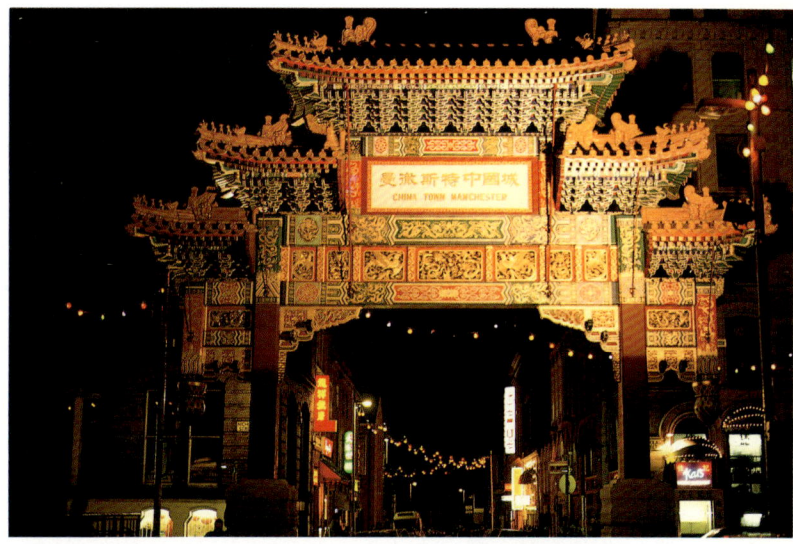

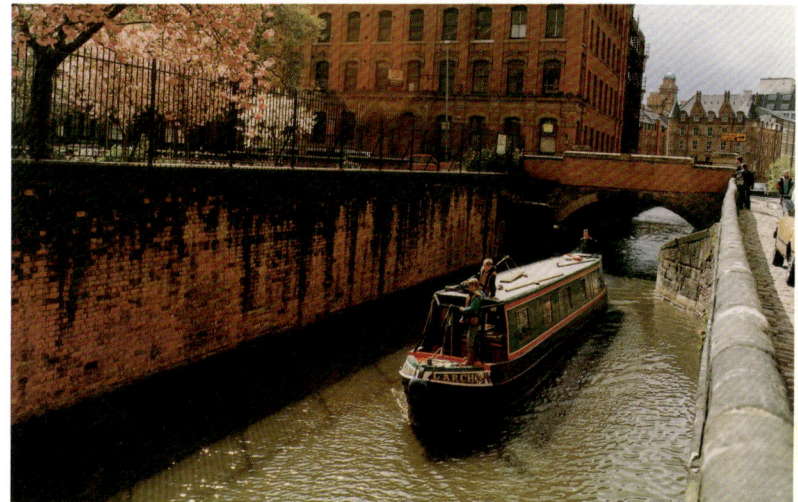

Canal Street to Piccadilly Village

You can see the smoothed stones of the canal wall here rubbed round by years of hemp ropes being drawn along them. Just to the left is the modernistic frontage of Manto Bar where you can get good food and drink both day and night. Back around the corner is Sackville Gardens, a good place for a sit in the sun - if it's sunny which it often is in Manchester because in spite of its nickname 'Rainy City' it has more sunshine than many another place. One of the sad things about the city, though, is that there are so few parks where people can sit out in the summer. Unlike London, our city fathers didn't have the foresight to keep areas of the town green and open, or perhaps land was at such a premium that leaving it as open spaces for the workers to get a bit of fresh air during their dinner breaks would have seemed sacrilege to these hard-bitten northern industrialists. However it is hoped that as the canal redevelopment takes place more areas will be set aside for people to sit, away from the traffic in 'car-free' zones. Canal Street itself has been made one way and closed off between Princess Street and Abingdon Street. There will be a piazza area outside the Union pub and trees planted to turn the area into a small urban park.

At the top end of Canal Street is one of the loveliest buildings in the city, the old Minshull Street magistrates courts, where the Italianate influence on the design is so strong you can imagine the building sitting comfortably in the Piazza Del Duomo in Florence or the rust-red Piazza of Siena. On the door facing you the two stone dogs, one on either side, could have come from any one of a hundred Florentine buildings.

The path drops back down to canal level here and then makes its way into the Undercroft, the longest stretch of tunnel on the walk, with above you the Joshua Hoyle building, London Road and 111 Piccadilly. There are the remains of old tunnels running from the Undercroft towards the old warehouses, and they and the noise from the lock gates make it feel as though you're walking through the set of *Phantom of the Opera*.

From the Undercroft the towpath rises up to daylight at Dale Street where there was once a vast network of waterways called Dale Street Basin. Sadly it is now nothing more than a car park and we leave the Rochdale canal here. At one time this area was the centre of the Rochdale Canal Company's operations and had more exposed water than Castlefield, but now the archway leading into the company's domain is all that is left of this once extensive complex. Our walk follows the towpath up to street level again, emerging through a very strange hole in the wall called the Horse Road, and here you have to go left and left again, crossing the road and passing by Jutland Street, the steepest hill in Manchester, to where the Rochdale meets the Ashton Canal.

An air of dereliction still hangs around this part of the city. Most of the arms of the canals have been filled in and turned into car parks, which is a pity, but there are plans to dig out many of these arms and to turn this area into something of a Little Venice; and when that happens it will be one of the liveliest parts of the city. The Jolly Angler just along the road is a great little Manchester pub and on the water just below you can see the Good Ship Creperie La Peniche, one time grain-barge *Claymore,* which has now found a new life as a wine bar and bistro. Paradise Wharf, just beyond La Peniche, is a self-funded development of offices and studios in the care of a co-operative of architects and designers with not much money but a great deal of vision.

20

Canal Street to Piccadilly Village

From Paradise Wharf we now follow a new footpath the last quarter of a mile to Piccadilly Village, where our walk ends. You could, if you wanted, carry on along the Ashton Canal to Droylsden with its Moravian Settlement and a whole other world of interest beyond. But all that is another book and our walk ends here, at the new Piccadilly Village, a development of waterside apartments and fascinating offices that like Castlefield is bringing life back into the city.

Close by here is an arm of the canal called Manure Wharf where dung from the Corporation stables and the 'night soil' from the earth closets of the area was collected. Before the days of flush toilets 'night soil men' came in the hours of darkness to empty every household's sewage from the privy and it was gathered at Manure Wharf and boated out to market gardens in Cheshire and Lancashire.

There is a story about the apocryphal Henshawes set on one of the manure boats that plied the canals at the end of the last century. They were a famous Manchester music hall act, the Flying Henshawes, and their motto, 'A smile, a song, a balloon and a safety net' appeared on billboards all over the North. But they were the last of a vanishing race, music hall was dying and bookings were thin on the ground when one day they were offered a week at Warrington Alhambra playing second on the bill to Enrico and his Whistling Ferrets. They were offered £20 for the week. They looked at the letter of offer glumly. Return fares to Warrington were ten shillings each, so with four of them that meant £2. Digs would be £3 each for the week - that only left £6 profit for a week's work.
Albert Henshawe had an idea.
'Fred Carter goes to Warrington from Ancoats Locks every week with a load of manure for the market gardens in Cheshire. We can get a lift with him for the price of his ale.'

So the next week the Four Flying Henshawes boarded the good barge *The Roaring Mouse* at Ancoats Locks and set off on their journey west. It was a hot summer's day and the cargo was nice and fresh so all four Henshawes sat on the pointed end upwind of the load.

At the first lock the lock-keeper shouted *'Ho bargee what load?'*

'Eighty ton of manure and the Four Flying Henshawes,' was the reply.

At the next lock the same cry rang between the dank walls of the warehouses.*'Ho bargee, what load?'*

'Eighty ton of manure and the Four Flying Henshawes,' again was the reply.

As they approached the third lock the eldest of the Henshawes, who had some pride in his calling, stepped to the stern and asked the bargee quietly,*'Mr Carter, do you think at the next lock we could possibly have top billing?'*

From Piccadilly Village you can retrace the walk the way you came or take the Metrolink back to Deansgate and Castlefield.

I hope you've enjoyed your day.

Mike Harding

New Life for Central Manchester

Improving the environment and promoting tourism and leisure are two important aspects of the work of the Central Manchester Development Corporation, which was set up by government in 1988 to revitalise 470-acres of rundown land and buildings next to the city centre.

The area runs in a swathe from Piccadilly through the Whitworth 'corridor' to Castlefield and beyond; and binding it all together are Manchester's 'hidden gems', the historic waterways on which much of the city's industrial growth was based.

The Development Corporation's task is to attract private sector investment into this fascinating, but until recently sadly neglected part of Manchester. Investment is and will continue to create new homes, new jobs and new leisure facilities, from hotels to carnivals.

To provide the incentive for such investment to flow into Manchester, a great deal of work has been necessary to improve the environment of the area. It covers a wide range of activities, from

simple but effective tasks such as repaving, street lighting and floral displays, to multi-million pound projects designed to renovate entire buildings - or canals.

One of the greatest challenges facing the Development Corporation was the restoration of the Castlefield Basin and the 'Rochdale Nine', the mile-long stretch of the Rochdale Canal, with its nine locks, that winds through - and sometimes beneath - the heart of Manchester.

It was in Castlefield that much of Manchester's history as a great industrial city began two hundred years ago, with first canals and then railways playing their part in the city's tremendous growth. In Victorian times they supported a vast infrastructure of buildings and trade, roads and transport, homes...and people.

But in this century Castlefield and the city's canals became disused and neglected, and in grave danger of being entirely abandoned with decaying buildings and overgrown wharves standing beside decaying canals, some of which were completely filled in.

Action to reverse the trend was started just in time, and today the canals and basins are enjoying a new lease of life, as the setting for a wide range of redevelopment projects.

The regeneration of Castlefield began in 1979, when Manchester City Council designated it as a conservation area; and in 1982 it became Britain's first Urban Heritage Park. In 1988 the Central Manchester Development Corporation started to build on the excellent work of the City Council to restore Castlefield and the canal network. This was to form an initial part of its early and continuing programme.

Castlefield was earmarked for tourism and leisure growth, based on the award-winning Museum of Science and Industry, the unique Granada Studios Tour and the Castlefield Hotel with its popular 'Y' leisure club. These three venues alone attract more than 3,000 visitors to Castlefield - *everyday*. On top of that, thousands more attend events such as the annual Castlefield Carnival, held each September.

Since 1988 the Development Corporation has spent some £5 million on the restoration of the Castlefield Basin and the Rochdale Canal in Manchester city centre, and work has also started on the Ashton Canal and Basin in the Piccadilly area. Much still remains to be done, but already the work has greatly transformed some important parts of central Manchester.

It has also encouraged developers to take a fresh look at the old buildings that sprang up during the canal age, from large warehouses to lock-keepers' cottages. As a result, a variety of imaginative schemes have been completed or planned, ranging from offices and leisure facilities to new homes - indeed for the first time in many years people are moving back to live in the area. Other new projects include an outdoor events area on a site opposite the Castlefield Hotel, and a visitor information centre.

Castlefield is the jewel in Manchester's crown. The Development Corporation has recognised the enormous potential of the area and has harnessed the commitment of private and public bodies to create the Castlefield Management Company.

This Company will aim to ensure that this fascinating area is cared for when the Development Corporation completes its own work in central Manchester. With it comes Britain's first 'urban rangers' whose job is to help visitors, organise events and generally look after Castlefield and its canals.

Wildlife

IRIS

GYPSYWORT

MICHAELMAS DAISY

Though the canals may give the impression of being sterile and dead areas there are many plants and animals that have made the waterways their habitat, due mainly to the purity of the water in the system when compared to the rivers which are still, in spite of tremendous efforts, heavily polluted.

Marsh plants such as wild angelica and gypsywort can be found along certain sections of the towpath as well as rosebay willowherb, Michaelmas daisy, Oxford ragwort and mouse-ear chickweed. There are flag iris and ferns along some sections of the banking while Canal Street has a self-seeded pear tree. Various pondweed and arrowhead (named after its leaf shape) can be seen in the clear open water and at the Bridgewater Canal end there are a number of species of coarse fish such as roach, perch and gudgeon.

It is hoped that by careful habitat management and by natural re-seeding the area will eventually become once more rich in flowers and wildlife. Small mammals will make their way along any wildlife corridor where there is food, and waterfowl will also make the area their home if there are enough nesting sites for them. The two swans and the handful of ducks are, we hope, just the beginning.

ROSEBAY WILLOWHERB

MOUSE-EAR CHICKWEED

OXFORD RAGWORT